I0824860

CHEERLEADING BASICS

Candice Letkeman

MEDIA ENHANCED BOOKS
AV²
BY WEIGL
ADDED VALUE • AUDIO VISUAL
www.av2books.com

Go to **www.av2books.com**, and enter this book's unique code.

BOOK CODE

AVX34936

AV² by Weigl brings you media enhanced books that support active learning.

AV² provides enriched content that supplements and complements this book. Weigl's AV² books strive to create inspired learning and engage young minds in a total learning experience.

Your AV² Media Enhanced books come alive with...

Audio
Listen to sections of the book read aloud.

Key Words
Study vocabulary, and complete a matching word activity.

Video
Watch informative video clips.

Quizzes
Test your knowledge.

Embedded Weblinks
Gain additional information for research.

Slideshow
View images and captions, and prepare a presentation.

Try This!
Complete activities and hands-on experiments.

... and much, much more!

Published by Lightbox Learning Inc.
276 5th Avenue, Suite 704 #917
New York, NY 10001
Website: www.openlightbox.com

Library of Congress Cataloging-in-Publication Data
Names: Letkeman, Candice, author.
Title: Cheerleading basics / Candice Letkeman.
Description: New York : AV2 by Weigl, [2019] | Series: Cheerleading |
Audience: Grades: K to Grade 3. | Includes index.
Identifiers: LCCN 2019012099 (print) | LCCN 2019014046 (ebook) | ISBN
9781791109844 (multi user ebk.) | ISBN 9781791109851 (single user ebk.) |
ISBN 9781791109820 (hardcover : alk. paper) | ISBN 9781791109837(softcover : alk. paper)
Subjects: LCSH: Cheerleading--Juvenile literature. | Cheerleading--United States--Juvenile literature.
Classification: LCC LB3635 (ebook) | LCC LB3635 .L47 2019 (print) | DDC 791.6/4--dc23
LC record available at https://lccn.loc.gov/2019012099

Printed in Guangzhou, China
4 5 6 7 8 9 0 28 27 26 25 23

022023
230206

Project Coordinator: Heather Kissock
Designer: Ana Maria Vidal

The publishers acknowledge Getty Images, iStock, Shutterstock, and Alamy as its primary image suppliers for this title.

CHEERLEADING BASICS

Contents

The World of Cheerleading

With cheers, jumps, and glittering pom-poms, cheerleaders are an important part of sports. These athletes pump up the crowd. Their routines dazzle fans. They cheer their teams to victory.

There are different types and levels of cheerleading. Most cheerleaders are in high school or college. Many middle schools have teams. Elementary schools do as well. **All-star** cheerleaders take part in national competitions. They typically do not cheer at games for sports teams. Professional cheerleaders work in major league sports. They cheer at National Football League (NFL) and National Basketball Association (NBA) games.

At games, cheerleaders usually repeat each chant three times.

A cheerleader's job is more than cheers and **tumbling**. Cheerleaders are leaders in their schools. They often help other students. Cheerleaders put on special events. They also lead pep rallies. Everywhere they go, cheerleaders are **ambassadors**. They represent their teams, schools, and communities. Cheerleaders are known for being hardworking and enthusiastic.

Many early cheerleading teams only had four to six members.

History of Cheerleading

Cheerleading started in the United States more than 120 years ago. Johnny Campbell was the first person to organize a crowd cheer. Campbell was at a football game at the University of Minnesota. It was 1898. He thought the team needed fresh energy. Campbell led fans in a cheer. He used words from their school song. He cheered, “Rah! Rah! Rah! Minn-e-so-tah!” The team won the game with the help of Campbell’s cheer.

The University of Minnesota still uses Johnny Campbell's first cheer.

Cheerleading has included both men and women. The first cheerleaders were men. They were called "yell leaders." Women joined cheerleading in the 1920s and 1930s. Soon, most cheerleaders were female. With more **athleticism** and competitions, cheerleading grew. By the 1960s, cheerleading was in almost every school across the country. All-star cheerleading began in the 1980s. Today's competitive cheerleading includes amazing displays of **stunts** and teamwork.

THE FOUNDING FATHER OF CHEERLEADING

Lawrence "Herkie" Herkimer is known as the founding father of cheerleading. Herkimer was a cheerleader in college. He went to Southern Methodist University in Dallas, Texas. He was there in the 1940s. Herkimer later started the National Cheerleaders Association. He also created a popular cheerleading move. It is now called the Herkie jump. He invented pom-poms and the **spirit stick**. He added gymnastics and new types of motions to cheerleading. His work helped make cheerleading more popular.

Herkie jump

Cheerleading Timeline

Cheerleading has changed in the past 100 years. First, only males were cheerleaders. Then, mostly females were cheerleaders. Now, the sport is **coeducational**. Magazines and movies have helped cheerleading become even more popular.

Megaphones became widespread in the 1940s.

1920s Cheerleading is an organized activity for males. They cheer at high schools and colleges in the United States.

1923 Women are allowed to cheer for the first time. They attend the University of Minnesota.

1956 Pom-poms with plastic streamers are invented. Older types were made of tissue paper. They were easily damaged.

1995 *American Cheerleading Magazine* is published. The magazine can be bought online and in print. There are four issues a year, one for each season.

2000 The hit cheerleading movie *Bring It On* is released. It stars Kirsten Dunst and Eliza Dushku. Five sequels are later made. They go directly to video.

2016 Cheerleading gets **provisional** status. Cheerleading could be part of the 2020 or 2024 Summer Olympics.

Kirsten Dunst

Most stunts need four or more cheerleaders.

How Cheerleading Works

A group of experts makes cheerleading safety rules. The group is called the American Association of Cheerleading Coaches and Administrators. School **squads** also set their own rules. These instructions focus on practices.

The U.S. All Star Federation sets guidelines for competitions. There are different rules for all levels of cheerleading. Many rules are about **spotters**. For safety, spotters need to be in specific places. Rules about tumbling and jumps are important. Certain types are not allowed. There are also special guidelines for coaches. All-star programs all have the same rules.

Some cheerleaders practice **six times** a week for two hours or more.

About 95 percent of all cheerleaders are now female.

Cheerleading Athletes and Coaches

Like other sports teams, coaches lead cheerleading squads. The coach's job is to teach **choreography** and routines. His or her duties include running **drills** and practices. The most successful coaches encourage and teach their cheerleaders. They inspire cheerleaders to do their best.

Coaches help cheerleaders stretch their muscles. Stretching keeps muscles strong and healthy.

A cheerleading squad includes different roles. The captain is the leader. The captain brings messages from the coach to the team. He or she often leads warm-ups. Captains organize team activities. They are positive and encouraging. For stunts, there are three main positions. The **flyer** and **base** work together. A spotter helps or catches the flyer.

Most cheer coaches have backgrounds in cheerleading or dance.

The Right Tools

Unlike many other sports, cheerleaders do not need much gear. Cheerleaders need athletic shoes. Uniforms are required for games and events. Practice clothing is also important.

Practice Clothing Most squads practice every day. Members need a few sets of practice clothing. Practice clothing is comfortable and tight-fitting. This way, cheerleaders can bend and move. Loose-fitting clothing can get caught. It can be dangerous when flying or tumbling.

Pom-poms Cheerleaders use pom-poms. Pom-poms get the attention of the crowd. They add sparkle and excitement to a routine. Pom-poms are usually in the team's colors. They are often shiny.

Uniform Everyone on the team wears the same uniform. Females often wear short skirts. Males usually wear long pants. Uniforms are typically in the school's or team's colors. Uniforms are tight-fitting and stretchy. This lets cheerleaders move easily.

Athletic Shoes The right shoes protect and support a cheerleader's feet. Cheerleaders usually have one pair for working out. They have a different pair for practicing stunts. Another pair is kept clean. These are for performances.

The Right Moves

All types of cheerleading include common jumps and stunts. Combinations of moves make routines unique.

High V and Low V In a high V, cheerleaders reach up and out diagonally. Arms are in the shape of the letter V. The shoulders are relaxed. In a low V, the arms are down diagonally. They make the shape of an upside-down V.

Tuck Jump In a tuck jump, cheerleaders jump up. They bring the knees as close to the chest as possible. The knees are together. The chest is kept straight up without leaning forward. The arms are held in a high V.

Back Handspring In a back handspring, cheerleaders start by standing. Their feet are together. They jump up and bend their back. Arms are thrown behind the head. Then, the cheerleaders flip upside-down. Their hands are placed on the ground. The legs kick up backward over the body. They land with feet and legs together.

Thigh or Shoulder Stand In a thigh stand, the flyer stands with feet apart on the thighs of two bases. The bases stand to the side. Their legs are held apart for balance. Each base holds one of the flyer's knees. In a shoulder stand, the flyer stands on a base's shoulders. The base holds the flyer's ankles.

Getting Involved

Cheerleaders are committed to being fit. They practice often and do their best at all times. Cheerleading is not easy. There are steps you can take now to get started.

Some squads start practice in the summer. This way, they are ready for fall sports.

1. Decide which type of cheerleading you want to do. You could be a cheerleader at your school. You would cheer at sporting events. Competitive cheerleading is another option.

2. Research the skills you need for the type of cheerleading you chose. You can ask the coach at school. You can do research online or at a library.

3. Get fit. No matter the type of cheerleading you like, it helps to be healthy. Being strong and having **endurance** is important.

4. Learn and practice moves and cheers. Ask a cheerleader you know to help you. He or she can teach you some basic moves. Try some of the moves from this book. Look up videos online. Always be sure to practice under adult supervision.

CHEERLEADING HANDBOOKS

Cheerleaders take their roles seriously. They follow their program's rules. This shows respect and responsibility. Most schools have cheerleading handbooks. A handbook is about the school's rules. It explains rules about uniforms and appearance. Guidelines for being at games and school events are also covered. First, cheerleaders must read the handbook. Then, they often need to sign a contract. The contract says they agree to everything in the handbook. See if you can find a local cheerleading handbook to read.

PROFILE

Lacey Henderson

Lacey Henderson had dreams of becoming a cheerleader. When she was 9 years old, she became sick. She had cancer in her knee. Her leg had to be amputated above the knee. Lacey did not let this stop her. She became a cheerleader. Soon, she was captain of her high school squad. Then, she won a college **scholarship** for cheerleading.

Lacey Henderson was given a basketball signed by the Denver Pioneers. It was in honor of her fight against cancer.

Lacey faced challenges as a cheerleader. Her **prosthetic** leg made jumps and tumbling difficult. Lacey worked hard to overcome these challenges. She found new ways of doing the moves.

Lacey left cheerleading after a while. Now, she competes in the Paralympic Games. Lacey encourages all young cheerleaders to have a positive attitude, believe in themselves, and know that anything is possible.

Lacey was in the 2016 Paralympic Games in Rio de Janeiro, Brazil. She came in eighth place in the long jump.

Quiz

1 Do All-star cheerleaders cheer at games for sports teams?

No

2 What percent of college cheerleaders are male?

About 50

3 What cheerleading tools did Lawrence Herkimer invent?

Pom-poms and spirit sticks

4 What organization sets guidelines for cheerleading competitions?

The U.S. All Star Federation

5 What are the three main positions for stunts?

Flyer, base, and, spotter

6 Should cheerleading practice clothing be loose or tight-fitting?

Tight-fitting

7 What does a base do during a shoulder stand?

Holds the flyer's ankles

8 What does Lacey Henderson do now?

She competes in the Paralympic Games.

Key Words

All-star: a type of cheerleading in which athletes compete during routines that include advanced moves

ambassadors: people who represent their groups

athleticism: an ability to do well at sports and physical activities

base: a cheerleader who tosses, catches, and supports other cheerleaders during stunts

choreography: how performers move during a routine, usually set to music

coeducational: including both males and females

drills: sets of practice moves that are repeated many times

endurance: an ability to keep going when tired or stressed

flyer: a cheerleader who is held up or tossed into the air when doing stunts

prosthetic: an artificial body part

provisional: temporary and likely to be changed if requirements are met

scholarship: money given to a student to help pay for his or her education

spirit stick: a long, thin stick or baton often decorated with ribbons and streamers

spotters: cheerleaders who watch flyers and catch them if they fall during stunts

squads: cheerleading teams

stunts: advanced cheerleading moves during which cheerleaders are held up or tossed in the air

tumbling: gymnastics moves, such as somersaults, rolls, and leaps

Index

Log on to www.av2books.com

AV² by Weigl brings you media enhanced books that support active learning. Go to www.av2books.com, and enter the special code found on page 2 of this book. You will gain access to enriched and enhanced content that supplements and complements this book. Content includes video, audio, weblinks, quizzes, a slideshow, and activities.

AV² Online Navigation

Audio
Listen to sections of the book read aloud.

Book Pages
AV² pages directly correspond to pages in the book.

Video
Watch informative video clips.

Embedded Weblinks
Gain additional information for research.

Key Words
Study vocabulary, and complete a matching word activity.

Try This!
Complete activities and hands-on experiments.

Quizzes
Test your knowledge.

Slideshow
View images and captions, and prepare a presentation.

AV² was built to bridge the gap between print and digital. We encourage you to tell us what you like and what you want to see in the future.

Sign up to be an AV² Ambassador at www.av2books.com/ambassador.

Due to the dynamic nature of the internet, some of the URLs and activities provided as part of AV² by Weigl may have changed or ceased to exist. AV² by Weigl accepts no responsibility for any such changes. All media enhanced books are regularly monitored to update addresses and sites in a timely manner. Contact AV² by Weigl at 1-866-649-3445 or av2books@weigl.com with any questions, comments, or feedback.